I0488852

Kindle Publishing Secrets Revealed

How Selling E-Books Allowed Me to Quit My Job and
Work Only Four Hours a Week

James Chen

Table of Contents

Learn to Make Money with Kindle Books

Passive income. We all want to make it. And publishing books on Amazon Kindle is a great way to do it. Imagine your books earning money 24 hours a day, 365 days a year on autopilot, leaving you the time to do whatever you desire. Sounds like a wonderful life, right?

It can be, and the first step is publishing your book. This book will guide you step by step through the process, from initial research to how to market your book.

Don't think you are a very good writer? I will show you how outsource your ideas to other writers who will write the books for you. All you need to do is publish them. And collect the checks.

I will also divulge a secret niche which sees extraordinary sales and searches on Amazon. There are very few writers taking advantage of this trick, and those who have are seeing their books in the bestseller lists. The best part: this niche only requires the books be between 15 to 30 pages in length. Short books, huge rewards.

Learn to take advantage of Amazon's enormous customer base, publishing books that will be searched for, found, and purchased. Learn to get your books to stand out from the millions of other ones already available in the Kindle store. It is simple: if people cannot find your books, they will not buy them. Learn how to be found.

The #1 Rule of Kindle Marketing

The rule is simple: find a process that makes money. And repeat it. Over and over again. This rule is particularly effective in terms of Kindle publishing. You publish your book, market it, let it make money, and do the entire process again.

Too many writers concentrate on one book. They invest all of their energy in making it perfect, trying to build up and audience, instead of writing additional books. Understand that having one book found within millions of books requires a whole lot of luck. But if you have two books, your odds increase. Think of each book as a lottery ticket, the more you have, the more likely you will have one hit the jackpot. Your goal should not be to have one book in the Kindle store, but hundreds. Don't imagine yourself as a writer, but as a publisher. And act accordingly.

Authors often focus on the visible success stories on Amazon, on the fiction writers who have sold hundreds of thousands of books. This is an incredibly small group, and their success is hard to replicate, because it was brought about by luck. You will most likely never get this lucky, so you need to create your own success. That means publishing a lot of books.

The people making money in the system are those who publish hundreds of books under different pen names. These books are often outsourced to a group of writers, as are the formatting and cover creation. This book encourages you to embrace the second method and act like a publisher, producing and selling as much content as you can.

Remember the more you publish, the larger your slice of the pie will be.

Fiction or Non-Fiction?

Here's my problem with writing fiction books: too many are being given away for free. Customers start to expect it, they become conditioned to getting free books. It then becomes difficult to sell to them, especially if the book is priced higher than 99 cents.

Non-fiction books are generally viewed differently. They are informative, and customers still believe that you need to pay for information. This is why the majority of books that I publish are non-fiction; I am able to charge a higher price for them.

You will learn that you want to price books in the Amazon sweet spot, which is between $2.99 and $9.99. Within this range, you will earn a 70% royalty; outside this range you only get 35%. The difference is royalties is considerable. For example, if you sell a hundred copies of a 99 cent book at 35% royalty, you will earn $35. But if you sell the same hundred books at $2.99 and a 70% royalty, you will earn about $205. Using the lower pricing point and 35% royalty ends up leaving a lot of money on the table that you could otherwise be pocketing.

But don't you sell more books at 99 cents? Yes. But you have to sell over 5 books at 99 cents to match the royalty earned on the same book priced at $2.99. And in my experience, this rarely happens.

Trying to publish a fiction book priced at $2.99 is a difficult task for a new writer without an established audience. The competition is just too fierce, and one romance novel isn't really that different from another.

Non-fiction books are much more specific, often focusing on a certain idea or concept. When a customer searches Amazon for this topic, we want our book to come up at the top of the search results. Assume your book is about making money online. Now, assume a customer searches for this term on Amazon. Your book comes up. The chances are very high they will click on your book, because it addresses the issue they were searching for. Contrast this with a customer searching for a romance novel. A whole list will come up, all of the books hard to differentiate, because romance novels are highly similar to each other.

The obvious point is that non-fiction is more easily targeted to its audience. There is less selling involved.

People have a problem, search to fix that problem, find a book that promises to fix that problem, and then buy that book. This is the reason why this book will focus on publishing non-fiction material. You will find it to be the easy field in which to make money.

You can still publish fiction books if you wish, I have quite a few. But understand that you will make more if you concentrate on non-fiction books. And we are in this to make money on Amazon.

Researching Your Book

Now that we have decided on publishing a non-fiction book, it is time to select a topic. Often the best place to start is with subject matter that you are familiar with. If you have expertise in a certain area and are open to writing the book yourself, you can always write in that area.

Don't be daunted by the task of writing; this is not a full length book that we are talking about. Instead, we want short guides within the range of 3000 to 10000 words. Most of my books are in the 5000 word range, which translates to about 30 pages of content. If there is a subject you are interested in and believe you can write at least 3000 words, I encourage you to do it. Writing your own book will save you money, and you may find that you enjoy the creative process.

But will it sell? This is a huge question and is where research comes in. The easiest way to find out what people are searching for on Amazon is to check out the auto-fill selections when you start to type in Amazon's search box. For example, if I type "how to", I get the following search suggestions:

"how to win friends"

"how to draw"

"how to write a book"

"how to stop worrying"

You then keep drilling down on these suggestions, offering up new search terms until you find one you wish to pursue.

Another method is to use the categories list on the sidebar in the Kindle Store. Searching by category is a great way to see different topic areas that are available to you.

Keep your topic selection related to solving problems, like weight loss or dating advice. Any topic that gives people advice is generally good, because customers are searching for this information. You are providing them with a service by giving them what they want. And this is the best way to understand what type of topic you should pick: are you giving the customer what they want? If yes, it is definitely a topic you should select.

Make certain to write down your topic keyword. Use the Amazon search suggestion feature to find other phrases used by customers that are related to your keyword. Write all of these phrases down. They are very important. You will eventually use them as your keywords when you publish your book. For example, maybe your main keyword is "cookie recipes". Related keywords might be "how to bake cookies", "dessert recipes", "cookie cookbook", and so forth.

You want to make certain that you have at least seven keyword phrases. These need to be things that people are actually searching for on Amazon. The better your keywords, the more search results your book will show up in, and the more customers your book will get.

The Perfect Title

You've come up with the perfect niche, you have at least seven keywords, now all you need is a title, one that will really sell your book. In non-fiction, the best titles are one that align well with the term the customer searches for.

So for example, if you are targeting customers who are searching for "how to lose weight", not surprisingly, the best title for a book would be "How to Lose Weight".

Using the keyword in your title has another enormous benefit, it will put you higher up in the search results. The same is true for using the keyword in the book description that appears on Amazon's page.

Don't get too creative with your title, the simple ones work the best. While you may think having a keyword for a title is boring, the payoff in search results and sales make it worth it. A lot of writers think they have hit upon the perfect title only to discover that no one is searching for that. And if no one is searching for your book, no one is buying it.

Remember that you are giving your customers what they want. If they want to learn how to lose weight, it is your goal to give them a book telling them how to achieve success. And to make that goal obvious from just reading the title. Your title needs to mirror what the customer wants, and using your keyword in the title is the best way to guarantee this.

A subtitle is also needed for your book. I always incorporate at least one other related keyword into my subtitle. For example, "weight loss" is a related keyword to "how to lose weight", so if I title my book "How to Lose Weight", I might give it a subtitle like "Weight Loss Made Simple". The point is simple: use as many keywords as possible to have your book appear in the widest range of search results. The more results your book appears in, the better the chance you have at making a sale.

If you follow these steps in finding a niche and keyword and basing your title and subtitle on your keyword research, you have taken the first important step in publishing a Kindle book that sells. Understand that they are many good books on Amazon that don't sell. Just as there are many bad books that sell a lot of copies. The difference: the bad books appear for terms that customers are searching for, while the good books remain buried deep within the results. If no one sees your book, I don't care how good it is, it will never sell.

Writing Your Book

Once you have a title, and an idea of what your book is going to be about, you can set about the task of writing it. Or—if you don't want to write it—have the book written for you by a freelancer.

Even if you decide to write your first book, I recommend that you become acquainted with outsourcing this type of writing work. Eventually as success comes, you will want to produce more and more books. You won't be able to write them all, that would take too long. So outsourcing and hiring freelancers becomes the only alternative.

Another benefit of outsourcing your book is that you can concentrate on marketing and selling your books. Remember that the goal is to be a best-selling author and not necessarily the best-writing one. There is only so much time available, so it is necessary to be efficient in how you utilize it.

Besides I can outsource a 5000 word book for $20. The time it would take me to write a book of that length is worth more than $20. Make certain that you value your time properly. If you enjoy writing, that's fine, just understand that at some point if you really want to increase your Kindle publishing empire, you will need to outsource work.

There are quite a few websites where you can outsource your writing jobs, but I'm only going to cover the three major ones, Fiverr, Odesk, and Elance.

Fiverr (http://www.fiverr.com) is the largest marketplace of sellers who will do a variety of different jobs, called gigs, for five dollars. Writing jobs are just a small slice of what you can find on Fiverr. In fact, we will also use Fiverr to have a graphic artist design the cover for our book.

If you go to the Writing and Translation section on Fiverr, you will see a slew of individuals offering to write a certain amount of words for five dollars. The way I do it is to go through the gigs, read the descriptions, and eliminate the ones who don't have a polished description. I will then contact the individuals on my short list and ask if they would be willing to tackle a larger project of 3000 or more words. And if so, what would the price be. Not all of the sellers will be interested, but you will find a few. I then pick the one who I feel can do the best job on my book. Usually I will ask if they feel comfortable researching and writing about the subject matter I decided to write about. Don't hesitate to ask questions, and pay attention to the responses, particularly to the writing. Is it good? Do you want this person to write your book? If you treat this process like a job interview, you will most likely come away with the best candidate.

The biggest plus of Fiverr is that the majority of sellers have English as their first language. You will not be outsourcing to someone who might not have the strongest grasp on English grammar. Now, this isn't to say that all the writers on Fiverr are good. That is far from the case. But there are some very good ones there, you just need to search for them. And when you find a seller who does a good job, reward them with more projects. Publishing a lot of Kindle books requires you to establish good business relationships with as many contractors as you possible can.

Now what should you pay? No more than $50. In fact, I don't like to pay more than $40 for a book to be written. The reason is simple: I don't want to have to wait too long for the book to turn a profit after earning its cost back. On Fiverr, it will likely cost you $40 to $50 to get a book written. That's okay, particularly since it is written by a native English speaker. To get anything cheaper, you will need to outsource the work to residents of another country. And the best site for this is Odesk.

Odesk (http://www.odesk.com) is very similar to Fiverr in terms of the different categories of services being offered. The biggest difference is that it is a job posting site. You will post your job for a writer and people will apply for it. Sounds easy, right? It is, as long as you follow a few basic steps.

Job posting is easy, but you want to make certain that you are clear on what you expect in your job description. Tell them that you need a writer for a non-fiction book which needs to be between 3000 and 10000 words. Odesk allows you to set a fixed price for the job, and I recommend that you do. You will get responses if you set the budget at $20, but the higher you raise the price the better your responses will be. Most contractors apply within the first day with a cover letter and how much they are willing to accept to do the job. The screening and interview process is by far the most important, so these are the tips that I use to weed out the pretenders from the contenders.

Because you will get non-native English speakers applying for your job, you will want to screen them much more carefully. I always ask to see samples of their writing. I also ask a lot of questions, because I want to see how they respond. This is what you have to look out for: they show you beautifully written samples, but their messages to you don't show the same level of writing skill. These individuals you want to avoid as they are likely going to plagiarize the content they give to you. Some will just change words here and there and try to pass it off to you as original. Be very careful and vet your writers thoroughly.

If the contractor writes very good English in their answers to you, this is the type of person you want to hire. There are some very good non-native English writers on Odesk, but it definitely takes work to find them.

Now this doesn't make Odesk sound great, so why would we use it? The price. I can often get a 5000 word book written for $25. It won't necessarily be the best quality, but it will be more than good enough. Personally, I get the majority of my books written by contractors on Odesk. There are a few who always do a great job for me, so I tend to keep them busy. Once again, it is about building business relationships; if you find someone good, hang on to them and keep them working.

Elance (http://www.elance.com) is a job posting site similar to Odesk, but with more contractors based in the United States and Canada. It is a good second option if Odesk doesn't work out for you. Elance also lets you set a budget on your job postings, and I recommend that you do it. You will get a large variety of applicants, many of them quite good. And also quite expensive. It isn't unusual to have a contractor quote hundreds of dollars to write a 5000 word book.

And this is the greatest issue with using Elance. It just costs too much. You don't want to have to sell hundreds of copies of the book just to break even. You want to make money, and spending too much money on producing your books is a sure way not to see a profit for a while.

Understand that your goal should be to get the best quality books written for the cheapest price possible. Produce your titles cheaply. It requires some work to find people who can produce quality content for a cheap price, but this is a task you only have to do once. Once you find enough contractors to create all your content, producing books becomes an extremely simplified process. And this is why cultivating these business relationships with your best contractors is vitally important. Their work will build your publishing business.

Creating the Perfect Cover

You know the saying don't judge a book by its cover? Forget about it. Amazon shoppers clearly do. A great cover can sell a terrible book. But a terrible cover won't sell your book no matter how good it may be. So you need a cover that pops.

Fortunately, this isn't as difficult as it sounds. What it boils down to is that you want the keyword that you are focusing on to be readable when it shows up in the Amazon search results. This means that the title needs to be clear and visible to the customer. If you have that with a clean, professional look, your book will sell. Guaranteed.

Remember that you are giving your customers what they really want. And what they really want is answers. If a book's cover promises this in big, bold letters that will be attractive to them. It will be the solution that they are searching for.

While you can use either Elance or Odesk to hire a graphic artist to design your book cover, I don't recommend that. It will end up costing you more than you need to spend. Instead, we will use Fiverr.

Go to Fiverr and do a search for "book covers". The search should return a bunch of gigs. You may see both 3D and regular book covers offered; you definitely want to purchase a 2D flat regular book cover. I suggest taking the time and going through the various gigs, looking through each artist's portfolio. Find someone who you feel can match your vision for the cover.

You don't need to pay more than $5 for a cover; you don't need any of the fancy extras like the original file formats. When you contact the seller, you want to make certain that you specify that the cover is for a "Kindle book". Amazon has size requirements for the cover, the largest size has to be a minimum of 1000 pixels. The majority of Fiverr cover designers know this, so they will size your book cover appropriately if you tell them this information.

A word of advice. I went through quite a few cover designers on Fiverr until I found one who produce the kind of covers that I was looking for. If you can, it may be a good idea to hire a few designers to design your cover and pick the best one. Since each gig only costs $5 a pop, it is not too great of an investment. And the payoff of finding a really good designer will make it totally worth it in the long run.

Preparing Your Book

Your contractor has finished writing your book and has sent you the Word document. Now what?

I suggest reading over the document, checking for errors and spelling mistakes. With spell check this should be a relatively easy process. You will also want to insert a title page at the beginning of the document. On this title page, you should put the title, the subtitle, and the author's name. Keep it simple; there is no reason not to.

After the title page is where I normally put my copyright page. This could be as simple as writing "Copyright (Insert Year) by (Author's Name or Publisher's Name)". It isn't a problem if you don't have it, but it does add to the professionalism of your book.

A table of contents is another nice touch to add. In Word, you can go to the References tab, select the Table of Contents drop-down menu, and then select Custom Table of Contents. This will open up a dialog box. You want to make sure that you uncheck "Show page numbers" before hitting OK. The table of contents will then auto-generate itself using the headings of each of the chapters. If the headings are not showing up, check that the chapter titles are actually in the "Heading 1" style. If not, change them and re-generate your table of contents.

Once I have a few published books in my library, I like to place previews of these books at the end of my newest books. Usually I will have the first chapter as a preview. Think of this as the perfect opportunity to sell your reader on more of your books. I often put two free previews at the back of my book, as well as a listing of all of my titles with clickable Amazon links.

Once the title page and any extras you desire have been added, it is time to convert the document to a format that can be upload to Kindle Direct Publishing. The first step is to save your Word document as a "Web Page, Filtered".

The next step is to download and install the Kindle Previewer:

http://www.amazon.com/gp/feature.html?docId=10007 65261

Start the Kindle Previewer and load your manuscript in the Web Page, Filtered format. The Kindle Previewer will automatically convert your book into the needed format. It is that simple. It will also give you the opportunity to see how your book will look on a Kindle. Go through it quickly to make certain you don't have any glaring formatting issues.

You now have everything you need to publish your book in the Kindle Store.

Publishing Your Book

If you haven't set up an account on Amazon's Kindle Direct Publishing, you need to do that now. Go to http://kdp.amazon.com to sign up. Once you sign up, you will be given access to your bookshelf. Since you have not published any books yet, it will be empty.

Since we are adding a new book, we want to click on the "Add new title" button. On the first page, you will enter your book's details. The first box asks if you want to enroll your book in KDP Select, check yes. This allows your book to be borrowed by Amazon Prime members. The best part: you will get paid for it. It is a great source of additional revenue.

Next, enter your book title and subtitle that you determined as part of your initial research. Unless the book is part of a series, leave the next box unchecked. I usually leave the edition number and publisher boxes blank, but it really is up to you. There is no benefit one way or the other.

The description is very important. You want to take your time here. This is the where you want to really sell your book. Focus on your keywords and make certain that they are in your description. Try to write as much as possible; you don't want short descriptions. I've noticed that my books that have the longer descriptions seem to sell better than books with shorter descriptions. Don't worry about the description being perfect, you can always change and revise it later if necessary after the book is published.

Next, add the contributors to your book. I suggest using a pen name. If you publish enough books, you will want a separate pen name for each genre. Always remember that when customers search for your pen name, all your books will appear. If they are related, the chances of an additional sale increase. If they are not related, you may lose credibility in the eyes of that customer.

Indicate your book's language and publication date, if you wish. You can ignore the ISBN box unless you have one; you don't need one, though. Under the Verifying Your Publishing Rights, you will want to select "This is not a public domain work and I hold the necessary publishing rights."

Selecting categories is another important step that you want to take your time with. Here is my suggestion: search the Kindle Store for your main keyword. Click on the first book in the search results. Go down to the book's details. You will see a ranking in the paid Kindle Store. Underneath this ranking, you might see additional rankings on the bestseller lists in various categories. If that is the case, note these categories and use them with your book. If the book doesn't have these rankings, keep searching the results until you find a book that does.

You want to select a category that does not have a lot of competition for the bestseller lists. Getting on the bestseller lists is the key for increasing your book's visibility. The good news is that you can tweak this until you find a related category that you can get listed on with little competition.

In the next box, enter the seven keywords that you uncovered in your research. Now, upload the cover that you outsourced as well as the book file that you produced using the Kindle Previewer. Do not worry about digital rights management; if people are going to pirate your book, digital rights management won't stop them. After you have uploaded both your cover and book, click Save and Continue to go to the pricing page.

The pricing page is much simpler, only requiring a few pieces of information. You want to check 70% royalty and enter a price of $2.99 in the box for the Amazon.com store. The other stories will automatically calculate their price in their currency based on the Amazon.com price.

I suggest checking the box that allows users to lend their book to others; it doesn't hurt and it allows you to build your potential audience. Once you agree to Amazon's terms and conditions, you can then proceed to publish your book. It takes approximately 12 hours for your book to become available in the Kindle store.

Congratulations! You have just published your first Kindle book. To check your sales, you can go to the Reports tab on the Kindle Direct Publishing website.

Getting Reviews

Positive reviews are definitely important in selling your book. They offer social proof; customers will often pick a book with a hundred positive reviews over one with only a few reviews.

While reviews are important to the success of your book, they are not nearly as important as some authors seem to believe. I have many books that had no reviews sell much better than books with quite a few reviews; reaching a certain audience will sell more books than reviews often will.

The point is not to stress out about reviews. Particularly bad reviews. There will come, and it is easier to ignore them than to get worked up about them. The hardest part about reviews is getting them.

Most new authors have no idea how difficult it is to get reviews of their work. They figure that if they sell a few books, or offer a free promotion, the reviews will pour in. This is far from the truth. Reviews are rare. You might have to have a thousand people download your book for free to get even one review. And that is far from guaranteed. Most of the people who buy or download your book will not take the time to review it.

That can't be right, you say. You see books with lots of reviews on Amazon. How do they get their reviews?

And this is where the dirty little secret in Amazon's review system is uncovered. A huge amount of the book reviews you see in the Kindle Store for self-published books are either by friends or family members or were purchased. Most of the self-published authors who have been successful on Amazon like John Locke have bought reviews. A lot of reviews.

It is important to understand that fake reviews is truly how the system works. That's not to say that real reviews don't happen, just that they are rare. Understand that this is more an issue with self-published books. The traditionally published books have a larger audience base, with many who actually do review books. Indie authors don't have this luxury.

So this leaves you with a decision: do you wait for reviews to appear organically or do you purchase reviews for your books? If you decide to purchase reviews, you can go on Fiverr and search for "book reviews". There are many sellers offering positive reviews for $5.

If you do purchase reviews, you want to make certain you buy a verified review. A verified review is one in which the reviewer purchases your book and posts a review. Verified reviews carry a heavier weight when Amazon calculates their search results. The easiest and most cost effective way to get verified reviews is to purchase your reviews during one of your books free promotions.

Understand that purchasing reviews or soliciting reviews from friends or family is against Amazon's guidelines. Amazon has the right to remove the review if they think it is suspect. Furthermore, reviewing another author's work in exchange for them reviewing yours is also against the guidelines. It is important that you are aware of this in making your choice.

Because of the inflated review system, you want to make certain that your book has at least an average of

4 stars. Anything less will likely impact your sales. If you are finding that you are getting bad reviews, you will want to think about having your book revised to increase its quality. Another option is to purchase five star reviews which will raise your book's average.

What it comes down to with getting reviews is deciding whether you want to purchase reviews or not. It is a question of ethics. Realize that your competition is likely buying reviews, so waiting for reviews to appear organically for your book will likely see you losing ground and potential customers.

The Perfect Niche

This chapter is going to introduce you to one of the most profitable niches for Kindle books on Amazon. This isn't a regular niche, but rather a very specialized type of book. These books sell incredibly well, because they piggyback on the notoriety of other books.

Remember when you were in school and your English teacher would assign a book for a book report. If you were like me, you probably didn't read the book. Instead, you used one of the various Notes's guides that summarized and analyzed the book. This audience still exists to this day; they have just grown up.

This is the demand that you will satisfy. And you will do it by basically writing book reports of current non-fiction or fiction bestsellers.

Let me explain. A customer searches for the newest hot book on Amazon, the search results return the book as well as your summary book. Often the customer will notice the price difference between the two. The regular book is likely over ten dollars, while your book is less than 5. This alone gets them to click on your book. Your summary book piggybacks on the popularity of the regular book.

So what should our summary involve? Imagine you are writing a book report, summarize the chapters, detail the characters, and add your own thoughts. Make it at least 3000 words, and you have just created a bestselling Kindle book.

If the name of the book you are making a reader's guide for is "Title X", you want to title your book "Title X Reader's Guide". Add a subtitle like "A Summary and Analysis." It is important that you don't hide the fact that your book is a reader's guide. Make certain that information is prominent, because you don't want to fool people, you just want to offer them a less expensive, cheaper alternative.

Publishing reader's guides for popular books is very lucrative. Particularly because the audience is huge. It's not unusual for these reader's guides to make $20 or more a day during the height of a book's popularity. Just imagine you had ten of these reader's guides and were pocketing $200 a day. Not bad, right?

There is a drawback, though. Reader's guides tend to earn big profits up front, but earn less and less as the book they are based on starts to wan in popularity. This means that you have to constantly put out new guides for other books to maintain a steady stream of income.

Diversification is key to using this method. You want to publish books as outlined in this guide that will be steady earners. You can then supplement these with reader's guides. The combination of the two can bring tremendous monetary rewards to you.

If you decide to publish a reader's guide, follow the steps as outlined in this book. Everything works the same, the title of your book will just tap into a much larger market.

Another trick to tap into a popular book's audience is to give one of your books the same title, but a different subtitle. You do need to be careful not to try and pass yourself off as the book; it is generally safer to be in a different genre, or to have a clearly distinguishable difference in subject matter.

I have seen this tactic employed a few times, and it has never failed in raising the sales rank of the book that is cashing in on the more popular book's title. And it isn't because you are fooling people, it is because you are reaching a much larger search audience. The point is to get your book in front of as many customers as possible. The more customers who view your book, the more who will eventually buy it.

Marketing Your Book

How to market your Kindle book is a broad topic. Many books could be written on this subject. The method outlined in this guide doesn't rely heavily on marketing, so I'm only going to cover a few tips that will be helpful.

After publishing your book, you will want to set up a free promotion of it for a day. This is a great way to get your book moving in the system. When you enroll in Kindle Select you are allowed to give your book away for free for a total of five days. You can take all the days at once, or space them out of the course of 90 days.

Never run a free promotion for more than a day; you want to sell the book, not give it away. If you are buying reviews for your book, you want to schedule them to coincide with your free promotion so you can get the verified option.

There are quite a few sites that will promote your free book if you submit the information. Most of them need you to submit the information days in advance. This will definitely get you more downloads and a higher ranking in the Free Kindle Store, which increases your exposure even more.

You can also write up a press release for your book (or hire someone on Fiverr to do it) and submit it to press release sites. The benefit of this is that your press release may eventually find itself indexed by search engines. This potentially allows more customers to eventually find your book.

Just as there are sites that promote free Kindle books, there are many that promote 99 cent books. If you want to jumpstart your sales, you can lower your price to 99 cents for a limited time and promote it on these sites. This is essentially a short term solution only, and not particularly effective.

Another option is to have a seller on Fiverr create a book trailer for your book, and then you can post it to Youtube. This is a great way to get indexed into the search engines. Want to get more views and likes to your video, use social media exchange site like http://www.like4like.org. These sites allow you to build up credits by liking other pages, and then spending those credits on having people view and like your page. It is a great way to increase the popularity of your social media page quickly.

You can also use this technique with Facebook pages and Twitter accounts. One effective use is to run your free promotion, tweet about it, and then use a social media exchange to get your message retweeted. I've been able to achieve some amazing reach employing this technique.

Your marketing should be entirely focused on building up your audience. That way when you do make an announcement, it will have the greatest impact. You don't have time to build your audience personally, responding to every tweet. You need to be able to build your audience fast and with little effort.

Final Word

You are now ready to tackle the wonderful world of Kindle publishing. All the tools you need to be successful have been given to you. The trick is keep publishing more and more books, always giving yourself a better chance to sell more books.

The tip alone on the lucrative nature of reader's guides should give you a great head start if you choose to go that route. Never forget that luck plays a large role in whether a book is successful or not. But here is the good news: you can make your own luck. Following the suggestions in this guide is gives you the best chance to ultimate succeed as a Kindle book publisher.

Good luck. And happy publishing.

Preview of "Cellulite Reduction: The Ultimate Guide on How to Get Rid of Cellulite" by Emily V. Steinhauser

What is cellulite in the first place?

As mentioned, cellulite is normal fat or may also be additional fat that is found underneath the connective layers of the skin. The unsightly lines and furrows on the skin develop as the fat pushes against the skin.

Cellulite is more common in women than in men simply because females have more fat tissue compared to their male counterparts. This is because of the difference of fat distribution in a woman's body compared to men. Cellulite may also be present no matter what body type you are which means even thin people have it. Finally, having cellulite does not mean that you are fat it's just that your body is more prone to develop it than other people.

Interesting cellulite facts:

If your parents and other family members have cellulite there is a huge possibility that you will also develop cellulite too.

There are so many reasons why a person develops cellulite, in women; hormones may play a huge role.

You can hardly see cellulite in people with dark skin color but it is still there.

Liposuction is one of the oldest but still effective ways to remove fatty layers on skin however the American Academy of Dermatology cautions about liposuction. They say that it only worsen the appearance of cellulite since the procedure may only create additional depressions on skin.

The best way to remove cellulite is careful planning. This involves a combination of the right diet, exercise, lifestyle changes and the use of effective treatments.

Prevention may help reduce the development of cellulite and prevention also includes diet, exercise and lifestyle changes.

Your dermatologist and your doctor are the best sources of information regarding the removal of cellulite.

What are the signs of cellulite?

First of all you need to spot cellulite to be able to plan how to get rid of it. The common places that you can find cellulite are parts of the body where excess fat usually deposit. Thus you may find cellulite on the thighs, the hips, buttocks, upper arms, on the midsection and sometimes on the neck area. Skin may appear

- Dimpled and uneven

- With obvious irregular marks on the surface of the skin

- There is discoloration along the area especially when viewed under natural light

Knowing the signs of cellulite will help people develop the ideal cellulite removal plan. Since cellulite may be reduced, if not removed, with the use of exercise, the ideal exercise regimen to tone the area with cellulite may be done.

I hope you enjoyed this free preview of "Cellulite Reduction: The Ultimate Guide on How to Get Rid of Cellulite" by Emily V. Steinhauser.

Preview of "Texting Secrets Revealed" by Vin Petrillo

Chapter 1 – The Approach

What is the "Approach"? In a typical pickup scenario—say in a bar or nightclub—the approach refers to making first contact with your intended target. This usually means approaching them and striking up a conversation. Simply stated, there are a ton of theories about the most effective way to approach a woman.

If you struggle with this portion of your game, I suggest reading pickup books that deal with this topic. While each may give you specific techniques, the overall takeaway will be to improve your approaches you must practice. The more experience you get, the better.

This applies equally to text dating. Practice is essential. I've noticed on of the big differences between the two is shy guys feel more comfortable texting than a real-world approach. This highlights a problem which needs to be overcome if you wish to have success in attracting girls: being shy. Nothing ruins your chances more than being shy. If you want to be successful, you need to face your fears straight on.

Most people fear public speaking. They often feel like they are being judged; that any mistakes they make are a personal reflection. Approaching girls magnifies these feelings. It becomes extremely personal. But this is a mistake; it isn't personal. It is not a reflection on you. If a girl rejects your pickup attempt, understand that is snap judgment. She doesn't know you; she doesn't know what the correct decision. She can only make a snap decision. Don't confuse the two.

One of the best life lessons that I ever got was to learn to embrace failure. You have likely heard the quote: that which does not kill you, makes you stronger. It's true. Failure breeds strength.

Pretend you are stuck in a maze. You wander around trying to find the exit. Every dead end that you encounter guides you closer and closer to the exit. By making wrong turns, you are able to discover the one true path. Dating is similar. Making mistakes will lead you to the path of success.

If your heart pounds and your hands sweat on an approach, take a moment and examine the thoughts that are controlling these feelings of fear. Ask yourself: what is there to be afraid of? Failure? Now ask yourself: is failure a bad thing? Or could it be a good thing?

Imagine you approach an attractive girl in a bar and you blow it; you get rejected. That sucks, right? Obviously this girl is the greatest thing on two legs, right? You feel like getting rejected is a bad thing. Later on, you discover this girl has a serious drug problem; she is a flake and steals from the people closest to her. How do you feel now? Maybe like you dodged a big, fucking bullet.

Realize that keeping perspective is always important. Understand that on the approach both parties are working with imperfect information. Your hope is that hooking up with this hottie will be a good thing. Instead, it might be the most catastrophic event in your life. The same thing applies to her.

The point is to stop looking at your results in the light of good or bad. That just screws your emotions up. If you believe you lost something good, you will feel sad.

Just as if you lost something bad, you would likely feel relieved.

So don't automatically equate failure with bad. Just like taking the wrong path in a maze is not bad. It just lengthens your journey.

Having the right mental attitude is an aspect that most dating advice books avoid. They will tell you to practice your approaches, but never offer any advice on how to conquer any fears you have. To control your fears, you need to show yourself that they are unfounded. Do not let yourself be fooled by your thoughts. Getting rejected and failing—at anything—is not automatically a bad thing; it can be a good thing. Just like turning down the wrong path in a maze is not inherently bad. Making mistakes helps us find the correct path.

If you still find yourself struggling with approaching people, take an acting class at the local community college or through a university extension program. Acting is wonderful for strengthen your presence and verbal abilities. Some students find it incredibly helpful also, because pretending to be a character in a play makes a social situation like approaching a beautiful girl less daunting. At the very least, acting classes can help you fake it until you make it.

While this is not the type of approach meant in text dating, it is helpful advice in improving your ability to approach women. The benefit should be obvious. The more women you approach, the more numbers you get. And the more girls you can text. Simply stated, if you don't approach girls and get their numbers, you aren't going to have any one to text.

But what about the texting Approach, namely sending that first text? I will discuss the case in which you have never met the person previously. The rest of this book will discuss texting girls you already know (though all of it also works for girls you don't know yet, too).

Say you are looking to message a girl. You saw her profile online, maybe on a dating site or social media site, you think she is cute and want to get to know her. What should you message her?

Understand that getting responses in these types of situations can be difficult. One of the best ways that I have discovered to elicit a response is to act like you have information that she would want to know. One example of this is as follows: you message her, "I can't believe you put that on your profile. How did you not get banned?"

Most girls read this, and their curiosity gets the better of them. They are confused and want to know what you are talking about. They also don't want to have anything embarrassing on their profile. Most will message you back wanting to know what you are talking about.

Your reply should be short: "You are in the middle of meeting a deadline, and you will get back to her later." The point is not to have an answer, but to make initial contact. After this, wait a week and then contact her normally. Don't bring up your initial message; forget it. Let her bring it up if she remembers, then ignore it. Just plow ahead, run your game.

Making contact like this should be the rare case. Don't expect tremendous success employing this type of cold-reading messaging. If this is your entire game, you need to work on approaching girls and getting more numbers. Understand that cold-reading messaging is similar to a telemarketer calling random people; there is a low probability of success. On the plus side of these cold-reading approaches is that you can experiment a lot, trying a variety of ideas without much effort. I suggest typing up your script in Notepad and copying and pasting in message boxes. Realize that this is a machine gun approach to texting, you will eventually hit a target if you shoot enough bullets.

Now that I've talked a little about approaches, the rest of the book will examine the nitty-gritty of text dating.

I hope you enjoyed this free preview of "Texting Secrets Revealed" by Vin Petrillo.

Other Books Available From Gamma Mouse Media

Below you will find other popular Amazon bestsellers from Gamma Mouse Media.

25 Tips to Improve your Text Dating Game – Aidan Upton

Knee Pain Treatment – Emily V. Steinhauser

Quiet – Amelia Austin

Lust for Me – Amelia Austin

Text Dating Secrets Revealed – Vin Petrillo

Cellulite Reduction – Emily V. Steinhauser

The Quick Start Guide to Macarons – Lindsay Stotts

Speed Reading Training – Warren R. Sullivan

Memory Enhancement – Warren R. Sullivan

Text Dating – Vin Petrillo and Aidan Upton

The Quick Start Guide to Perfect Pancakes – Lindsay Stotts

Stormy Passions – Shad Gable

www.ingramcontent.com/pod-product-compliance
Lightning Source LLC
Chambersburg PA
CBHW071633170526
45166CB00003B/1320